ROCKFORD PUBLIC LIBRARY

3 1112 020121477

W9-BJL-403

J 796.32309 W119 D649
Doeden, Matt
Dwyane Wade : basketball
superstar

102015

WITHDRAWN

ROCKFORD PUBLIC LIBRARY

Rockford, Illinois

www.rockfordpubliclibrary.org

815-965-9511

DWYANE WADE

Basketball Superstar

BY MATT DOEDEN

ROCKFORD PUBLIC LIBRARY

CAPSTONE PRESS
a capstone imprint

Sports Illustrated Kids Superstar Athletes are published by Capstone Press,
1710 Roe Crest Drive, North Mankato, Minnesota 56003.
www.capstonepub.com

Copyright © 2014 by Capstone Press, a Capstone imprint.
All rights reserved.
No part of this publication may be reproduced in whole or in part, or stored in a retrieval system, or transmitted
in any form or by any means, electronic, mechanical, photocopying, recording, or otherwise, without written
permission of the publisher or, where applicable, Time Inc.

Sports Illustrated Kids is a trademark of Time Inc. Used with permission.

Library of Congress Cataloging-in-Publication Data

Doeden, Matt.
 Dwyane Wade : basketball superstar / by Matt Doeden.
  pages cm.—(Sports illustrated kids. Superstar athletes.)
 Includes bibliographical references and index.
 Summary: "Introduces readers to the life of pro basketball star Dwyane Wade"—Provided by publisher.
Cataloging-in-publication information is on file with the Library of Congress.
ISBN 978-1-4765-8599-4 (library binding)
ISBN 978-1-4765-9429-3 (paperback)

Editorial Credits

Nate LeBoutillier, editor; Lori Bye, designer; Eric Gohl, media researcher; Eric Manske, production specialist

Photo Credits

Getty Images: Alexander Tamargo, 10; Sports Illustrated: Bob Rosato, 2–3, 5, 6, 16, Jeffery A. Salter, cover (left),
John Biever, 12, 15, 22 (top), John W. McDonough, cover (right), 1, 19, 21, 22 (middle & bottom), 23, 24, Manny
Millan, 9

Design Elements

Shutterstock/chudo-yudo, designerpix, Fassver Anna, Fazakas Mihaly

Direct Quotations

Page 7, from June 21, 2006, *USA Today* article "Heat Beat Mavericks to Win NBA Title" by David DuPree, www.
usatoday.com

Page 20, from June 21, 2013, *USA Today* article "Dwyane Wade aka 'Three' Soaks Up Win, Next Comes Rest" by
Jeff Zillgitt, www.usatoday.com

Printed in the United States of America in North Mankato, Minnesota.

092013   007771CGS14

TABLE OF CONTENTS

CHAPTER 1

FINALS HERO

Miami Heat **guard** Dwyane Wade was on fire. It was the 2006 National Basketball Association (NBA) Finals between the Heat and the Dallas Mavericks. The series was tied at two games each. Dallas led by four points with three minutes to go in Game 5. That was when Wade took over. He scored from inside and outside. He hit shots from the free throw line. Then he knocked down a jump shot with just two seconds left to tie it. Overtime!

guard—a basketball position; guards are usually responsible for dribbling the ball, passing, and shooting from outside

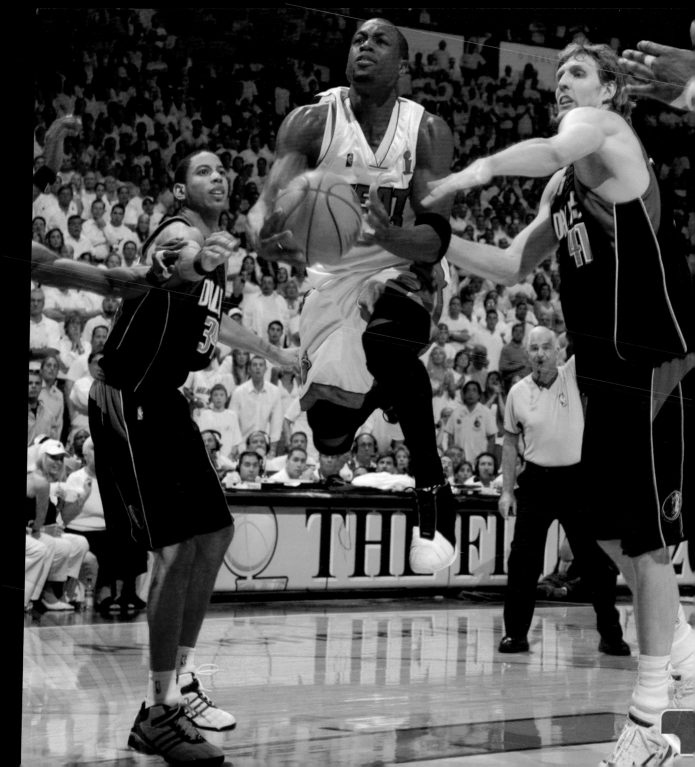

Dwyane Wade (left) and teammate Shaquille O'Neal celebrate Miami's 2006 NBA championship.

In overtime Wade was fouled and stepped to the free throw line with two seconds to go. He calmly made the first shot to tie the game at 100. Wade knocked down the second free throw as well. After the Mavericks missed a shot, the Heat won the game, 101-100. Then Miami finished off Dallas in Game 6. The Heat were NBA champions, and Wade was named NBA Finals MVP.

"I don't want to say I put the team on my shoulders. We did it as a team. [My teammates] gave me the opportunity by putting the ball in my hands."
—Dwyane Wade on winning the 2006 championship

CHAPTER 2

THE EARLY YEARS

Dwyane Tyrone Wade Jr. was born January 17, 1982, in Chicago, Illinois. He lived the early years of his life with his mother in a tough Chicago neighborhood. At age 8 he moved in with his father in nearby Robbins, Illinois. There Wade discovered his talent for basketball. He dreamed of being like his basketball idol, Chicago Bulls superstar Michael Jordan.

Chicago Bulls guard Michael Jordan

Dwyane Wade and and his sister, Tragil

varsity—the highest level of
competition in school sports

In high school Wade showed promise as a wide receiver on the football team. But his first love was basketball. Wade wasn't even on the **varsity** basketball team as a sophomore. But by his junior year, Wade was the star of the team. He averaged 20.7 points per game. Then as a senior, he averaged 27 points.

SISTERLY INFLUENCE

Dwyane Wade's older sister Tragil was a guiding force in Dwyane's childhood years. As adults they began working together on Dwyane's charity foundation.

Dwyane Wade in his Marquette days

Wade accepted a **scholarship** to Marquette University in Milwaukee, Wisconsin. He had to sit out his first year while he worked on his studies. But it was worth the wait. In his second season, he led Marquette all the way to the 2003 NCAA Final Four. As one of the nation's best players, Wade was named to the All-America First Team. After the season Wade announced that he was entering the NBA **Draft**. The Miami Heat picked him fifth overall.

scholarship—money provided for a student's education
draft—an event at which professional teams select new players

CHAPTER 3

NBA STAR

Wade scored 18 points in his first NBA game. He went on to have an excellent **rookie** season in 2003–04. His great all-around game helped the Heat reach the second round of the playoffs. He only got better in 2004–05. He averaged 24.1 points per game and made the All-Star team. The Heat reached the Eastern Conference Finals.

rookie—a first-year player

Dwyane Wade (left) and veteran teammate
Eddie Jones during Wade's rookie season

Wade and the Heat were even better in 2005–06. Wade's amazing performance in the playoffs led Miami to its first NBA championship. Wade also became a key player on the United States Olympic men's basketball team. He was Team USA's top scorer in the 2008 games and led the team to the gold medal.

In 2010 Wade helped convince fellow stars LeBron James and Chris Bosh to join the Heat. Reporters called the trio of All-Stars the "Big Three." The Heat, led by the Big Three, made the NBA Finals in 2010–11, only to lose to the Mavericks. But in 2012 they beat the Oklahoma City Thunder to win the NBA title.

SENSE OF STYLE

Wade has become almost as famous for his clothing as for his play. He loves to wear brightly colored suits during the playoffs. In 2006 *GQ* magazine named him the NBA's best-dressed player.

CHAPTER 4

BUILDING A LEGACY

Wade added to his **legacy** when the Heat won the championship again in 2013. The series went seven games before the Heat beat the San Antonio Spurs. With his **clutch** all-around performance, Wade proved once again that he was one of the greatest players in the NBA.

"[T]onight I just wanted to take a minute, take a moment and just soak in being a kid from Robbins, Illinois, from Marquette University, and now having three championships."
—Dwyane Wade after the 2013 NBA Finals

legacy—the accomplishments for which a person is remembered

clutch—able to perform one's best in the most important games or situations

TIMELINE

1982—Dwyane Wade is born January 17 in Chicago.

2003—Wade leads Marquette to the Final Four; the Heat select him fifth overall in the NBA Draft.

2004—As a rookie, Wade leads the Heat to the second round of the Eastern Conference playoffs.

2006—Wade is named NBA Finals MVP as the Heat defeat the Dallas Mavericks.

2008—Wade wins an Olympic gold medal with the United States men's basketball team.

2009—Wade averages 30.2 points per game to lead the NBA in scoring.

2012—The Heat win the NBA championship over the Oklahoma City Thunder.

2013—The Heat win the NBA championship for a second straight season, this time over the San Antonio Spurs.

GLOSSARY

clutch (CLUCH)—able to perform one's best in the most important games or situations

draft (DRAFT)—an event at which professional teams select new players

guard (GARD)—a basketball position; guards are usually responsible for handling the ball, passing, and shooting from outside

legacy (LEG-uh-see)—the accomplishments for which a person is remembered

rookie (RUK-ee)—a first-year player

scholarship (SKOL-ur-ship)—money provided for a student's education

varsity (VAR-sih-tee)—the highest level of competition in school sports

READ MORE

DiPrimio, Pete. *Dwyane Wade*. Hockessin, Del.: Mitchell Lane Publishers, 2012.

Sandler, Michael. *Dwyane Wade*. New York: Bearport Pub., 2012.

INTERNET SITES

FactHound offers a safe, fun way to find Internet sites related to this book. All of the sites on FactHound have been researched by our staff

Here's all you do:
Visit *www.facthound.com*
Type in this code: 9781476585994

 Check out projects, games and lots more at
www.capstonekids.com

INDEX